PUNDEMONIUM

PUNS ARE EVERYWHERE!

Lewis and Clark upon seeing the Pacific Ocean

BY HARVEY C. GORDON

ILLUSTRATIONS BY FRANK CORONADO

The Punster's Press

CREDITS
Illustrations for the front cover, the PUNdemonium Pun Collection (Section I) and certain puns in the Punster Proficiency Test (Section III) are by FRANK CORONADO. Illustrations for some puns in Section III of the book are by RAND KINGTON and by DAVID LEVI where credit is indicated.

Copyright © 1983 by Harvey Charles Gordon

Published by:

The Punster's Press
3834 Joanne Drive
Glenview, Ill. 60025

Printed in the United States of America
First Printing: July, 1983

Library of Congress Catalog Card Number: 83-61419
ISBN: 0-9601402-2-0

PREFACE

Puns are everywhere! The world is in a state of PUNdemonium. More than ever before puns are popping up in television and radio commercials, business slogans, advertisements, greeting cards, headlines for newspaper articles and TV and motion picture entertainment. Puns are featured regularly in popular columns of major newspapers. My first two puns books, *PUNishment: The Art of Punning or How to Lose Friends and Agonize People* and *Grime and PUNishment: A Collection of Sexciting Puns*, have been discussed on TV and radio programs around the country and have been the subject of numerous feature articles in major publications. In my opinion, we are in the midst of a golden age of puns, the likes of which has not been seen since the Shakespearean era.

To survive and flourish in this world of puns it is important to know how good you are as a punster. That is why I have created the PPT—the Punster Proficiency Test (not because I am a testy person.) The PPT is designed to test your pun-ability and rate your skills as a punster. This is your chance to have fun measuring your proficiency with puns and seeing how you compare with other punsters.

PUNdemonium is divided into three sections. The first section of the book contains a collections of new puns, a number of which are favorites of punsters around the world. The second section contains examples of the numerous puns we are exposed to in the mass media, in advertising by consumer-oriented businesses and in the field of entertainment. The third section of the book is the Punster Proficiency Test, which will determine how good the reader is with puns and separate the true artist from the mere amateur.

I believe that my first two pun books have contributed to the popularity of puns and have helped attain overdue recognition and appreciation for the pun as an important form of humor. Hopefully, a large number of readers will enjoy the challenge of taking the PPT, demonstrate a high level of proficiency and then strive to improve their pun-ability. If this occurs, *PUNdemonium* will have gone an important step further in developing and expanding the noble art of punning.

Table of Contents

Preface

I. PUNdemonium Pun Collection

II. Puns Are Everywhere!

III. The Punster Proficiency Test

I. PUNDEMONIUM
PUN COLLECTION

INTRODUCTION

The following collection is made up of my most recent puns and puns that have been provided to me by punsters all over the world. From the time my first book, *PUNishment,* was published in 1977, I have received numerous letters from fellow punsters who enjoyed my books and wanted to share their favorite puns. In addition, while promoting both *PUNishment* and *Grime and PUNishment,* I appeared on TV and radio shows around the country with audience participation. On several of these programs a record number of phone calls were received during my pun segments. I have included some of these puns in the collection.

As before, I have organized my pun collection by subject matter for easy reference and quick association. Many of the categories used will be familiar to readers of *PUNishment.*

I would like to take this opportunity to express my appreciation to all those punsters who have taken the interest and made the effort to share their favorite puns with me.* It is gratifying to know how many people all over the world enjoy and use puns and contribute to making punning a widespread art and important form of humor.

---

* Unfortunately, it has not been possible to give credit to individual contributors due to the difficulty in determining a pun's source or originality. On a number of occasions the same or similar puns were sent to me or called in by different contributors.

ANIMALS

Where do sheep get sheared? At the bah-bah shop, of course.

Skunks are able to avert danger by using their common scents and instincts.

A farmer would rather contend with a small boll weevil than a large one because it's the lesser of two weevils.

You could describe two spiders who just got married as newly webs.

People who rub down ponies have reoccurring throat problems. They're always feeling a little hoarse.

Horse trainers have learned that the best way to make a slow horse fast is to take away his oats.

I read about a sophisticated mousetrap device that lures mice into the trap with soft music. It plays a catchy tune.

You might describe a cow that has just given birth to an offspring as de-calf-inated.

Termites were apparently unaware of the Tylenol scare last year. They continued to eat through bathroom floors —tile and all.

THE PERFORMING ARTS

A young actor from Indianapolis auditioned for a part in a television sitcom and favorably impressed the producer and director. They jokingly remarked, "Hoosier agent, kid?"

When it comes to buying groceries, actors are not prudent consumers. They prefer a small roll to a long loaf.

I understand there is a new British porno movie coming out soon with the title of *Loins of London*.

An actress was hired for the lead in a play about Joan of Arc. However, she ended up getting fired.

A talented private in the army was ordered to sing at a benefit show by his company commander. It was a command performance.

A rumor that Miss Piggy of the Muppets was going to do a nude bubble bath scene in an upcoming movie turned out to be a lot of hogwash.

People who have met Rich Little in Las Vegas say he makes a good first impression.

There have been actresses through the years who have used the "couch and cast" system to "make" their way to the top.

At a Halloween party last year my wife wore a bunny costume and I dressed up as Lou Costello. Together, we were rabbit and Costello.

Another writer and I were going to do a takeoff on the movie *Airport,* but the project never got off the ground.

When I went to see the play, *1776,* I wore lots of cologne because I knew the play was about colonial times.

One might describe a labor union for orchestra members as a group of musicians acting in concert.

I understand that a number of deodorant companies wanted to sponsor the television program, "Ascent of Man."

A musician got mad at his wife for putting his saxophone and violin on top of their TV set. He told her there is enough sax and violins on television.

BUSINESSES, OCCUPATIONS AND PROFESSIONS

Inept tailors tend to be neurotic. They're always repressing things.

Many real estate brokers like to negotiate purchases and sales of their clients' property at coffee bars of restaurants so they can always make counteroffers.

A business school graduate landed a great job with a coffee company right out of school. He was offered an excellent salary and all the perks.

Many people in the monogram business achieve initial success.

A former employee of an executive search firm now buys lettuce and other salad items for a large restaurant chain. He's still considered a head hunter.

People who make automobile retreads are not very ambitious. They're always ready to retire.

Once a person gets his barber's license, he will do his best to get a head.

When sugar company executives travel overnight on business, they always stay in suites.

The owner of a flower shop was shaking after being held up by an armed robber. You might describe the man as a petrified florist.

A friend of mine worked for a tennis ball manufacturer for six months before getting canned.

A securities firm realized that one of their young employees was not destined for a career on the International Monetary Market when he bought a huge quantity of hot dogs instead of Swiss Francs.

I heard about an enterprising young woman from Alabama who wants to form a telephone company in her state and name it after herself. She would call the company, "Southern Belle."

When two police demolition experts were called in to disconnect a time bomb in a city building, one man said to the other, "Wire we doing this?"

A photographer for a popular men's magazine was recruited by an income tax service. He's familiar with all the right forms.

You might say that a real estate developer who likes to see his name on new office buildings, even if they can't be rented, has an edifice complex.

I read about a inventor who is developing an automatic packaging machine to be used at check-out counters in food stores. If it works, he's sure to make a bundle.

Some farm workers like receiving a portion of the raisins they produce as compensation because they always want to get a raisin pay.

You might describe the head of the bicycle manufacturers association as the spokesperson for the industry.

When young sportswriters start out in Chicago, they often cover baseball at Wrigley Field as Cub reporters.

It is not the post-game locker room interviews that are enticing women to become baseball reporters. We all know that diamonds are still a girl's best friend.

Who always falls asleep at a corporate board of directors meeting? The bored members, of course.

The owner of a country and western bar hired an engineer to build a mechanical bull for his club as soon as possible. The engineer said he would get right on it.

A popular country and western singer asked a Jewish real estate broker about mansions for sale in Beverly Hills. The broker replied, "Funny you should mansion it; do I have a house for you."

The best place to buy electrical appliances is at an outlet store.

Nothing is more important for a boat captain than to be recognized among his piers.

When an automobile mechanic was given the ax by his employer, he decided to open his own chop shop.

I understand that a number of house painters belong to the Church of Ladder Day Saints.

A friend of mine invested his life savings in a muffler shop that didn't work out. You might say he exhausted his resources.

Years ago when a woman made a career out of the navy, she became a permanent Wave.

I know a promiscuous female stockbroker who makes sure that all her male clients get their share.

In order to purchase a shipment of goose feather jackets from the manufacturer, a department store had to make a down payment.

Sometimes life for a lens maker can be a real grind.

Two Brothers decided to leave their monastery and open a fish and chips restaurant. One became the fish friar and other became the chip monk.

I understand that railroads require new conductors to train extensively for their jobs.

The union steward at an automobile manufacturing plant was investigating a complaint that an employee was fired for taking a brake.

All publishers have book that are bound to do well.

The camera is used extensively in various types of businesses. You might say it lens itself to many uses.

A real estate developer built tiny condominium units for midgets. To help sell the project quickly, the developer offered six months free rent to anyone who signed a purchase contract. He advertised the development as "Stay Free Mini Pads."

I heard rumors that before the company chose the name "Mr. Steak" for their restaurant chain, they rejected the name "Miss Steak" (for obvious reasons.)

A punster from upstate New York informed me that the broker who sells mobile homes in his town is called a "wheel estate broker."

Radio DJ's have a tendency to refer to bus boys as dish jockeys.

A nudist decided to stop at a tailor shop on the way home. The perplexed tailor saw him and said, "Sew what?"

Most carpenters are nervous individuals. They're always biting their nails.

Snow plow operators are very perceptive people. They always get the drift.

A shoe store that is owned by one individual would be called a sole proprietorship.

Most successful businessmen will tell you that what counts most in business is an adding machine.

DOCTORS AND DENTISTS

My wife and I went to visit a married couple, who are both psychiatrists, at their new house. To make them feel at home we brought them the perfect housewarming gift—an assortment of nuts.

The best place for a psychiatrist to put someone in a hypnotic trance is Transylvania.

Psychologists concede that the tennis court is one place where love means nothing.

A few years ago when office space was very tight, a group of optometrists was forced to occupy an old, run-down office building. It was truly a sight for sore eyes.

An optometrist got tired of working in New York and decided to move to the Aleutian Islands in Alaska. You might say he became an optical Aleutian.

A number of eye doctors live to a ripe old age. They often dilate.

I know an internist who gives complete examinations to hundreds of patients every year. He considers December 31st the end of his physical year.

A friend of mine used to make a lot of jokes about proctologists until he needed painful hemorrhoid surgery. Now, he doesn't make any more cracks about the subject, and is glad the surgery is behind him.

A paramedic passenger on a train was awakened in the middle of the night to help deliver a baby in the sleeping compartment. It was an upper birth.

Three rheumatologists decided to merge their practices into a medical group specializing in arthritis. You might describe the merger as a joint venture.

Some people think that a rheumatologist is the person who passes out rooms at the front desk of a hotel.

I know an oral surgeon who always plays the same refrain from the song, "Over There," before pulling a tooth— "The Yanks are coming, the Yanks are coming."

A guru refused to allow his dentist to give him any novocaine even though he had a number of bad cavities. He wanted to transcend dental medication.

Dentists appear to be depressed quite often. They're always looking down in the mouth.

A Japanese man called his dentist's office to schedule an appointment for his bad toothache. When the receptionist asked about the nature of the problem and when he could come in, the man replied, "Tooth hurty", to which the receptionist replied, "How about three o'clock?"

There is a suburb south of Chicago which has to be the ideal place for a dentist to set up practice. The name of the town is Flossmoor.

A friend of mine has gone to the dentist ten times in the last four months. He's thinking about putting his dentist on retainer.

As soon as I arrived at the endodontist's office for root canal work, I lost my nerve.

Many people would prefer that doctors and dentists use a word other than "practice" to describe what they do, even though they realize that practice make perfect.

One of our clients is an oral surgeon. He claims to be Jewish by extraction.

Many photographs taken in hospitals are x-ray-ted.

FISH AND FOWL

A friend of ours told us a gruesome shark story for the second time last night. However, the shark grew some since we first heard it.

Many migrating birds view an empty birdhouse along the way as a cheep hotel.

An eccentric man once harnassed a number of carrier pigeons to the front bumper of his car to pull it out of the mud. You might say the man was pigeon towed.

When a farmer discovered that a number of his chickens had escaped through broken chicken wire, he tried to re-coop his losses.

FOOD AND DRINK

A lawyer from my office and I were walking through the gourmet food section at Marshall Field & Co. when a young lady approached us with a tray of complimentary cheese samples. When my friend asked what kind of cheese she had, the lady replied, "Edam." I said, "Okay, we'll eat'em."

Some friends of ours are doing extremely well in a candy-producing venture. They're making a mint.

A few weeks ago we had a bad meal at a new German restaurant. The appetizer was terrible and the wurst was yet to come.

Many brides and grooms request that a certain type of soup be served at their wedding in order for their marriage to be consommé-ted.

We once went to a farmer's market where bushels of corn were being auctioned off. There were lots of auction-ears.

A friend of mine, who used to eat a sandwich and French fries for lunch everyday, is now on a diet and will only eat potatoes one day a week—on Fri-day.

When my wife and I visited Honolulu a couple of years ago, we went to see Pearl Harbor, had a few drinks and got bombed.

When some friends took a major league umpire to a new sandwich shop and asked him if he ever had an Italian beef, the umpire replied, "Yes, when I called him out on strikes."

A liquor store that wants to conserve energy will put the lites out in its beer section.

I heard about a man who carries a flask of liquor in a carved-out portion of his bible. He refers to his nip on the way to church as his bible belt.

The favorite dessert of most carpenters and boxers is pound cake.

A construction worker who is trying to lose weight will eat his lunch out by the street in order to curb his appetite.

A baker who messes up when he makes torts will have to bake a new batch and call them "retorts."

A new deep dish pizza parlor opened in the city with great expectations. However, the critics panned it.

AMERICANA

What university in Southern California describes what happens when the smog clears in Los Angeles?—UCLA, of course.

A few years ago when I was out West, I met some American Indians who belonged to one big Hopi family.

Many American women try to plan their pregnancies so they give birth on Labor Day.

I heard rumors that President Reagan puts pages from the *New York Times* on his floor to wipe his feet on rainy days. For him the newspaper is the *Times* that dry men's soles.

My first two books, *PUNishment* and *Grime and PUNishment,* have been very popular in Boston. You might say the books have had Mass appeal.

During my publicity tour for *PUNishment* a couple of years ago, I did a number of interviews in Washington, D.C. You might say I believe in Capitol PUNishment.

Another stop on my publicity tour was Cleveland. For some reason I had an Erie feeling the entire time I was there.

President Reagan is trying to transfer more spending authority to state and municipal governments under his "New Federalism" plan. He believes that the best way to trim the fat from federal spending is to shift to lo cal government.

A Jewish man from New Orleans ran into a Cajun friend of his from rural Louisiana and said, "How's Bayou."

Some Americans must wonder whether President Reagan's closest economic advisors are janitors when they look at his sweeping economic changes.

Allegedly, when Lewis and Clark finally reached the Pacific Ocean, Lewis exclaimed, "Eureka!" to which Clark replied, "You don't smell so good yourself!"

For many American settlers, peace with the Indians was just a pipe dream.

In *Gone With The Wind* the Civil War left Scarlett O'Hara's plantation in Terable condition.

The army is thinking about paying tribute to its early female soldiers by establishing a Wacs museum.

Many people believe that legalized gambling has made Atlantic City a bettor city.

I have a good friend named Ira. You might say that every bank account he has is an I.R.A. account.

I was told that working at the Board of Trade in Chicago is the pits.

Making someone from a warm climate spend a winter in Minneapolis might be considered cool and unusual punishment.

INTERNATIONAL

College students from the Republic of China don't get drunk very often, but once in a while they like to Taiwan on.

A man jumped off the Eiffel Tower with a parachute and landed in the river. The man was in Seine.

There were some contradictory statements made by the media about Prince Charles' wedding. I heard one newscaster say: "The royal wedding went off without a hitch."

Tourists in Egypt are usually senile people.

Viewers of the movie, *The Winds of War,* could see what a furor Germany created in the 1930's and '40's.

Some people have the mistaken notion that Robin Hood used a portable toilet back in 12th Century England because he never went anywhere without his Little John.

Sir Lancelot once had a bad dream about his horse. It was a knight-mare.

Former Iranian President, Bani Sadr, went through some rough times before he was able to escape from Iran. You might say that now he's Sadr, but wiser.

I heard rumors that on a visit to the United States Queen Elizabeth became quite upset with the musicians who were playing "Hail To The Chief" for the President. Supposedly, she said, "How dare you hail when I'm reigning!"

The angriest nation in the world has to be Ire-land.

When a well-known Scotish bagpipe player was asked whether a man can wear a kilt and still be masculine, the Scotsman tried to skirt the issue.

Many people who have visited Warsaw during the recent labor unrest have found the Polish capital to be a very striking city.

LAWYERS AND THE LAW

Juries must never be satisfied with their verdicts. They're always returning them.

The receptionist at our law office had two trays of file cards on her desk (one for active files and one for disposed files) and was updating the cards in the latter. I walked by and said, "I see you're in disposed now."

A personal injury lawyer I know told me that if his wife gives birth to a girl, he will name her "Sue."

If a judge wants to include "dicta" in his legal opinion, he will do it by using a dictaphone.*

An attractive English lawyer named Esther, who was working as a solicitor in London, decided to take a part-time job as a stripper at a nightclub in the city. She wanted to be a bare Esther.**

It's difficult to buy lunch for Czechoslovakian divorce attorneys. They're always asking for separate Czechs.

A contested hearing to determine heirship under a will might be described as a case of trial and heir.

---

* "Dicta" is a judge's statement of opinion on some legal point other than the principal issue of the case.

** There are two types of lawyers in England. A barrister is a qualified member of the legal profession who presents and pleads cases in court while a solicitor is not a member of the bar and may not plead cases in superior courts.

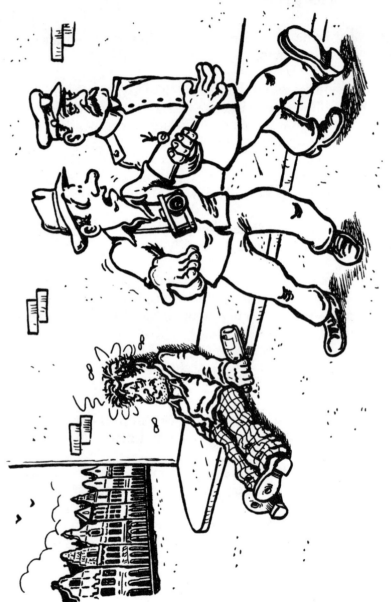

A person can be arrested in Prague, Czechoslovakia for walking past a drunk in the street. He will be charged with passing a bum Czech.

LOVE AND MARRIAGE

A man fell in love with a coalminer's daughter. He told a friend, "Someday I'm going to make her mine."

A woman fell in love with the doctor who performed her breast enlargement operation and decided to move in with him. However, after a few months they broke up, and all she had left were her mammaries.

Couples who are having marital problems should spend a weekend at a nudist retreat. It's a good place for them to air their differences.

A recent survey has disclosed that waterbeds are a major cause of divorce. They cause couples to drift apart.

Government economists are concerned that the rising divorce rate and deferred marriage plans will lead to stagnation.

Two nuclear disarmament demonstrators recently got married. You might say they met by chants.

A young lady sent her boyfriend a rainbow colored greeting card that read: "I Love Hue."

I know a very homely man who must be every woman's dream when it comes to kissing. Women who know him say, "What a kisser."

My sister has an attractive girlfriend who just moved here from Dayton. So far, she's not datin' anyone.

I heard about a woman who is married to an infertile English baron. She's not bearin' any children.

SPORTS AND RECREATIONS

When pitcher Jim Palmer has a bad night on the mound, the situation must remind him of one of his underwear commercials. He makes a brief appearance.

When Illinois Bell's softball team played the team from Commonwealth Edison, there were lots of utility infielders in the game.

The new owners of the Cubs decided to make popular TV announcer Harry Carey an attractive offer to lure him away from the White Sox. You might describe his signing as a "cash and Carey" deal.

When the White Sox acquired outfielder Rudy Law from the Dodgers last year, Sox general manager Roland Hemond lamented the fact that the Sox no longer had Jorge Orta. "Otherwise," he said, "we could have had Law and Orta."

When some clients accepted my invitation to go to the ball game the following weekend, I said I would touch base with them during the week.

I understand that old quarterbacks never retire; they just pass away. And old running backs never retire; they just get run down.

When the National Football League players were on strike last year, it looked like the Columbia shuttle flight was going to be the only touchdown of the Fall.

A friend offered me his football tickets for this week's game. However, I already had plans and had to take a pass.

Two old ladies brought a bottle of Scotch to the ball park. By the fifth the bags were loaded.

Before Detroit had a good football team, fans would become bored at the games. They would bring books and read between the lions.

An aspiring place-kicker accidently kicked a football through his neighbor's window. He had to foot the bill for the damage.

When the football coach started sketching a play on his blackboard, the players assumed it was a draw play.

Professional football players often tell the punters and place-kickers on their teams how soft their jobs are just for kicks.

A football player who continues to play after he is all washed up becomes a scrub.

At one of the home games during the disappointing 1981 Bears' season, someone hung a banner that read: "Chicago—Home of More Dog Teams than the Yukon."

When my brother goes to the Chicago Stadium to watch a hockey game, he can sit at the rear of the second balcony and still see all the action. He has good ice sight.

Professional basketball players always have enough money. They're never short.

A cross-country ski race will be held in Sweden shortly. The winner will be the first one to cross the Finnish line.

Many politicians get high from jogging because they're used to running on a platform.

An overweight male jogger was able to catch up to an attractive female runner long enough to say, "My pace or yours?"

I know a marathon runner who will only enter races with an uphill finish so if he doesn't win, he will at least be runner up.

Many successful waiters get a great deal of pleasure from playing tennis. They believe in service with a smile.

I have learned through the years that the laws of economics apply to tennis. After playing a couple of hours, one reaches the point of diminishing returns.

Professional bowlers must thoroughly enjoy their sport. They always have a ball.

A number of people who camp outside like to sleep on bedrock.

People who go hand gliding for the first time end up feeling soar all over.

Many dishonest merchants become avid sailors. They know how to rig a sale.

MISCELLANEOUS

Any woman who can spend an entire day at home without talking on the telephone should win the no Bell prize.

When a TV interviewer asked me to come up with a quick pun about my hat, I rattled off something off the top of my head.

Last weekend I spent three hours triming the shrubs around our house. When I finished, I was bushed.

One of the lawyers in our law firm, who injured his ankle playing tennis, was poking people in the office with his walking stick. He was constantly raising cane.

When I was in college in St. Louis, some fraternity brothers and I crashed a houseboat party on the Mississippi. You might say we unexpectedly barged in.

A young attorney was hesitant about staying home from work with a bad cold because he feared his bosses would think ill of him.

On my first day back in the office after a two-week vacation, I was at my secretary's desk when one of the lawyers approached me from the rear and said, "You're back." I turned around with my hand on my spine and said, "Why, yes. It is my back."

When a woman purchases hosiery, she does not want to get a run for her money.

I wouldn't be surprised if Anita Bryant thought that homosexual men should be arrested for male fraud.

At first there wasn't much action at the singles bar, but later, things started picking up.

A Chinese gentleman called in during a radio show to tell me about his friend, Mr. Wong, who noticed that his newborn son looked very Caucasian, and was quite perplexed since he knew that two Wongs don't make a white. (His wife could not convince him that Occidents will happen.)

It has been said that birthdays are like cheap underwear. They tend to creep up on you.

When informed that half of the members of the Governor's personal staff had come down with a strange illness, a reporter commented, "Maybe it's a staff infection."

A major northern city allocated a specific amount of money to purchase machines that could melt snow on city streets. The money was often referred to as a "slush fund."

When Sylvia Hanika defeated Martina Navratilova in the finals of the 1982 Avon Tennis Championships in New York, a Chicago newscaster commented, "Isn't it a little early for a Happy Hanukah."

One Saturday my wife and I had a great time shopping and having lunch at Marshall Field & Co. You might say we had a Field day.

A librarian told me about the time she selected a title for a patron who had asked for a critique of "Walden." When the patron inquired whether the work was fairly comprehensive, the librarian replied, "It looks pretty Thoreau to me."

A neighbor brought home an old telephone booth for his basement. The phone didn't work, but it was quite a conversation piece.

There is a person on the President's staff who is considered an expert on protocol. When a problem comes up, he knows which pro to call for the answer.

A woman who was close to a nervous breakdown successfully avoided mental illness by constantly sitting in a rocking chair. She never went off her rocker.

On a beautiful summer afternoon a country lawyer decided to take his boat to the lake. He left a sign on his office door that read: "Out to Launch."

When the fisherman was forced to sell his boat, he had no moor to look forward to.

A customer at my wife's bank mistakenly addressed the cashier of the bank as "Sam" instead of "Jim". A nearby employee was amused by the incident, and told the cashier, "You know, you really don't look like a Jim," to which he replied, "I hope I don't smell like one either."

Aging rabbis tend to get gray around the temples.

A abortion in Czechoslovakia might be referred to as a cancelled Czech.

Men who make obscene phone calls have sexual hangups.

Watching a blind man make his way through a nudist camp was a touching sight.

A mother who wants her small children to have Kleenex at all times will wash them every night.

Someone finally wrote a book about repairing your own clock. It's about time.

I was at a party recently where a man had a few too many drinks and did a takeoff of a male stripper.

A friend of mine saved money for a number of months to buy an expensive illuminated globe for his office. He said it meant the world to him.

When someone pays to have a chair recovered, their invoice should be receipted also.

A wealthy lady in New York enjoys the company of a certain cab driver and hires him to drive her around the city on many occasions. The cab driver refers to the woman as "My fare lady."

I was once talking to a group of people about a friend of theirs named "Charles" who they referred to as "Boris." When I asked if he was of Russian descent, they replied, "No. He just tends to bore us."

A lady in front of me in the ticket line thought that the "surcharge" on theater tickets applied to men only.

You might say that money spent on detergent to unclog one's kitchen sink is money down the drain.

A person who likes clean swimming conditions at the beach should swim when the ocean is tidy.

Some people have the mistaken notion that Robinson Crusoe invented the four-day work week because his work was always done by Friday.

Readers of gossip magazines will tell you that a maternity dress is just as revealing as a paternity suit.

We have learned that the person who organized the first mooning demonstration was a man named Seymour Butz.

I once received a Christmas card from someone with a picture of salt and pepper shakers that read: "Season's Greetings."

There is a high school boy who likes to sign the names of his friends under graffiti he writes on washroom walls. You might say he's always forging a head.

The morning after a violent wind and rain storm hit the city, debris from damaged trees was cleared by the Sanitation Department's branch office.

One can always tell a dogwood tree by its bark.

I have a friend who loves to be outside when it snows. He happens to be a flaky person.

Authorities realize that they would have trouble keeping Jewish people in jail because they eat lox.

There is a police detective who carries his revolver in his hat. You might describe the weapon as his cap gun.

The police receive many telephone reports of stolen automobile engines every year. However, a number turn out to be crank cases.

A woman once swallowed two contact lenses by accident. She is now known for having a great deal of insight.

Those unfortunate members of our society who cannot tolerate puns might view this book in the following manner:

II. PUNS ARE EVERYWHERE!

A WORLD OF PUNS

More than ever before the public is being bombarded with puns from consumer-oriented businesses, the mass media and the world of entertainment. To see how often puns are used to get our attention and amuse us, keep track of the puns you see and hear over the course of a week while watching television, listening to the radio, reading newspapers and magazines, and shopping for various goods and services.

The following are some examples of the puns I recall from business slogans, advertisements and commercials, newspaper headlines, TV sitcoms, motion picture comedies and nightclub entertainment in recent years. I have also included a few puns which undoubtedly will be used by certain businesses and professions in the future.

ADVERTISEMENTS, BUSINESS SLOGANS AND COMMERCIALS

A ladies' store in New York that sells speciality wool dresses had a pre-Christmas advertisement that read: "Make Your Presents Felt."

The pro at our tennis club is offering a special discount on lessons for the next two weeks. His bulletin board sign reads: "First Come, First Serve."

A Par 3 golf course just outside the city has lights for evening play. Its advertisement reads: "The Swingingest Night Clubs In Town Are Right Here."

There is a company in our community that makes kitchen cabinets to order which claims that its workmen are "professional counter fitters."

I remember a magazine advertisement for a certain brand of liquor that read: "Sip Into Something More Comfortable."

A certain laundry soap is advertised on television as being "the best detergent on American soil."

A company that makes chocolate chip cookies claims that, compared to the competition, their product is "the champion-chip cookie."

Joe Namath does a TV deodorant commercial in a professional football team's locker room in which he talks about how there is now more emphasis on defense and that there are less "offensive" players in the game.

Amtrak has a television commercial with the line: "America's getting into training—training the Amtrak way."

There is a pun-laden commercial for a local savings and loan association where the owners of a small bakery refer to the institution as "a great place to watch your dough rise."

Some time ago Continental Airlines did a number of commercials with the slogan: ". . . we really move our tail for you."

Dick Butkus and Bubba Smith do a golfing commercial for a certain light beer in which Mr. Butkus comments about how you shouldn't be too full if you're trying to get birdies. Mr. Smith replies, "Yeah. Those things move awfully fast."

There is another beer commercial with hockey great Gordie Howe in which a man approaches the bar next to him and asks for his "check". Mr. Howe proceeds to level the man with mighty body check.

McDonald's restaurants were once promoting their banana milk shake by saying the drink "has appeal."

A well known group of restaurants in the Chicago area is operated by a company called "Lettuce Entertain You."

A jeweler who does a lot of watch repair work has a sign in his window that reads: "We Work Over Time."

A neighborhood fireplace shop states in its advertisement that it has "everything the hearth desires."

A local flower-shop chain, which prides itself on carrying a large assortment of merchandise, claims it sells "every bloomin' thing."

A scavenger service has a phone book advertisement that reads: "Our Business Is Picking Up."

A very exclusive suburban beauty parlor claims to be "a cut above the rest."

A Chicago bank has a large downtown billboard that reads: "We Give Chicago A Lot Of Credit."

Another bank is trying to get its customers to rent safety deposit boxes that are "keyed to their needs."

A food store ran an ad for turkeys and other Thanksgiving foods that read: "Happy Holidays And All That Good Stuff."

A men's clothing company advertises that they're "the only ones that can suit you."

A roofer who claims to handle all types of jobs uses the slogan: "We top 'em all."

A suburban hotel that is trying to promote its banquet facilities has a roadside sign that reads: "Have Your Next Affair Here."

There is a nearby carpet dealer who advertises that he has "the best floor show in town."

The developer of a residential subdivision down the road claims to offer "a lot for a little."

A nearby auto dealer warns customers to "look before you lease."

A local rust-proofing company advertises that it won't let your car "rust in piece."

There is a suburban firm that claims to have "down-to-earth landscaping artists."

Here are some puns that I have not seen or heard yet, but which undoubtedly will appear in the promotion of various goods and services in the future:

One of our bank clients is planning to open a 24-hour safety deposit business. I suggested that they call their venture, "Lock Around The Clock."

A group of suburban obstetricians in a one-story office building will have a sign in their window that will read: "We Deliver."

There will be an English fertility specialist whose slogan will be: "If you're not begetting any children, we should be getting together."

A group of doctors that do face lifts and other cosmetic surgery will have the following business slogan: "If you're not becoming, you should be coming to us."

A crematorium that wants to have widespread appeal will use the slogan: "All men are cremated equal."

A company selling cemetery plots will have the slogan: "We'll be the last ones to let you down."

NEWSPAPER HEADLINES

The day the mercury dipped to 26 degrees below zero, the coldest reading in Chicago history, the front page headline for the *Chicago Sun-Times* read: "Have An Ice Day."

An article about a Harvard University study concerning the possible connection between excess coffee drinking and cancer had the following headline: "Coffee Study Causing Quite A Stir."

When a car smashed through the front window and entrance to a barber shop in Santa Barbara, California, while someone was getting his hair cut, the caption for a newspaper photograph of the incident read: "Haircut—And A Close Shave."

When a thief raided the White Sox spring training clubhouse in Sarasota, Florida, and stole six of Carlton Fisk's baseball gloves, the *Chicago Tribune* reported the incident with the headline: "Fisk Would Like To Get Mitts On Thief."

The caption for a sports article photograph showing a stiff body check during a National Hockey League game last December 31st was: "Smashed On New Year's Eve."

When UFO's were in the news, a syndicated columnist wrote a story entitled: "If UFO Landed, Would You Be Alienated?"

Last Spring I read an article about the popularity of Richard Pryor that had the title: "No Pryor Restraint —He's Making All Kinds of Movies."

This Summer a Chicago newspaper ran a story about local golf courses entitled: "Chicago Area Golf Courses Fit Golfers To A Tee."

A recent review of the best ice cream places in town was entitled: "The Scoop About Ice Cream Parlors."

The headline for an article about the place-kicker for the University of Illinois last Fall read: "Illini Kicker Puts Sole Into Game."

ENTERTAINMENT

In the movie, *Love At First Bite,* a spoof about Dracula, Richard Benjamin refers to the famous vampire as "a real fly-by-night character."

In one segment of the movie, *History of the World—Part I,* Mel Brooks plays King Louis XVI of France in 1789. When someone informs him that the people are revolting, he replies, "You're telling me. They stink on ice . . ."

"M*A*S*H" has been one of the most popular comedy series in the history of television. Episodes of the show are laced with puns. A few examples come to mind:

> When B.J. heard that someone had made derrogatory comments about the marines, he asked the person if indeed he had been "rotten to the corp."

> When an entertainer visiting the 4077th was introduced to Major Charles Winchester, he remarked, "You must be the big gun around here. I've always wanted to meet a person of your caliber."

> When someone came into "the Swamp" inquiring about the whereabouts of some missing underwear, B.J. told the person to "be brief."

> While eating crab legs at an outdoor picnic, Hawkeye suggested that a good way to end the war would be to shell North Korea with crabs.

(Ironically, in a humorous letter a couple of years ago Alan (Hawkeye) Alda told me that he was trying to get fewer puns on "M*A*S*H." He said, "It's not that I don't think the pun is a legitimate form of humor, it's just that I can't stand them.")

In an episode of "Love Boat" a man was posing as a widow's guardian angel. He told her that when he doesn't know what to do in a given situation, he just "wings it."

The TV show "Police Squad" had loads of physical reaction puns. One that I recall is when a police officer told a fellow officer to cover him, and the latter draped him with a blanket.

In an episode of "The Jeffersons," George and Louise accidently took a buggy with a Chinese lady's baby instead of their granddaughter. Upon realizing their mistake, Louise exclaimed, "We took the Wong baby! I mean we took the wrong baby!"

In the same episode, George showed his maid, Florence, a doll he had purchased for his granddaughter, and told her it was a "Florence doll" because "you wind it up and it doesn't work."

The moderator of the PBS program, "Wall Street Week", Louis Rukeyser, is a superb punster and very adept at working puns into serious conversations about the economy and stock market. For example:

> When an analyst was discussing some of the airline stocks, Mr. Rukeyser inquired whether he thought a particular stock was ready to take off.

> Another time, after an expert had completed his assessment of the photography industry, Mr. Rukeyser concluded the discussion by saying, "I think we've got the picture."

A number of popular comedians use puns in their nightclub and television routines. A well-known example is Henny Youngman's line: "Now, take my wife. Please! Take my wife!"

III. THE PUNSTER PROFICIENCY TEST

EXPLANATION AND INSTRUCTIONS

A pun may be defined as "the humorous use of a word, or group of words which are formed or sounded alike, but which have different meanings, in such a way as to play on two or more of the possible applications," or more simply as "a play on words." The Punster Proficiency Test contained in the following pages is designed to test your punability and measure your skills as a punster.

The Test is divided into five parts. Parts 1, 2 and 3 require you to complete puns by filling in missing words. In Part 1 a group of possible answers is provided to help you complete each of the puns. In Part 2 each incomplete pun has a corresponding illustration which will help you think of the correct answer. In Part 3 you are entirely on your own. There are no clues to help you figure out the word(s) necessary to complete each pun. Your skills as a punster are really on the line (the blank line).

Part 4 of the Test attempts to evaluate your ability to think on your feet and create puns on the spot. Hypothetical situations and dialogue are described in which the opportunity to blend a pun into the conversation arises. You are asked to come up with an appropriate pun for each situation in a limited amount of time. Also, Part 4 tests your ability to think of puns on designated subjects in a short amount of time. A good punster should be able to deliver a pun on practically any subject. I'm sure you remember the story about the punster in 18th Century England who claimed he could make a pun on any subject. When the king told the punster to make a pun about him, the man replied, "I cannot, Your Majesty. The king is not a subject." For that remark the punster was instantly banished from the kingdom. (A punster must always be prepared to make certain sacrifices for his puns.)

Part 5 of the Test is optional and is primarily geared for punsters with artistic ability. Puns which lend themselves to graphic design are provided and the punster is asked to produce the best possible illustration for humorously portraying each pun. However, as I have said many times, one does not have to be an illustrator to be an illustrious punster. A punster who is not artistically inclined can team up with a person who is and jointly create the illustrations for Part 5. The punster should be able to envision the illustration in his or her mind and be able to convey the idea to the artist. (This is what I have done for most of the illustrations in my three pun books.)

Part 4 is the only portion of the Test that has specific time limits. You may take as long as you like on the other parts of the Test and enjoy them at your leisure.

It is suggested that you fill in your Test answers with pencil so that after checking your answers, you can complete all the puns in Parts 1, 2, 3 and 4 in ink. Also, I suggest that if you are taking Part 5 of the Test, that you draw your illustrations on scratch paper first and then insert your drawings in the book.

As punsters are among the most honorable people in the world, I assume that no punster will look at the answers at the back of the book until he or she has completed the Test. Once all parts of the Test are finished (or the first four parts if you choose not to create the illustrations for Part 5), turn to page 98 to score your answers and evaluate your Test results.

And now turn to Part 1 and begin the Test.

PART 1

Complete the puns below by choosing appropriate words from the following list. There is one blank space for each missing word. (No word in the list should be used more than once. Some words will not be used at all.)

alter	materialistic	sell
barrel	meteor	shady
capsizes	mist	short iron
cleaners	money	spigot
date	newspaper	staggering
dedicated	paradox	stirrup
disguise	patients	stuffed
elicit	pear	subs
float	peas	sundae
full	petal	tie
green	press	to pay
hats	reserves	to spend
lightheaded	sand wedge	unbelievable
manors	scoop	unscrupulous

EXAMPLE:

Under stress a good doctor will not lose his _patients_.

1. People who work in the garment industry tend to be _____.

2. The activities director at a Colorado resort tried to _____ some interest in horseback riding.

3. There are vendors in front of the train station every night who try to _____ flowers.

61

4. In recent years some respectable-looking passengers on international flights have turned out to be terrorists in _____.

5. As soon as a golddigger "spots" a wealthy man, she's ready to take him to the _____.

6. The coach told his talented, 150-pound running back that before he could become a star, he first had to become a little _____.

7. The word "_____" could be defined as two medical practitioners.

8. Never go sailing with a haberdasher; all they talk about is _____.

9. During recent labor negotiations, the president of the tailor's union tried to get a lot of _____ coverage.

10. Two silkworms were once having a race. However, they ended up in a _____.

11. A dense fog in our area is causing a number of accidents on the highway. When the fog clears, it won't be _____.

12. If I can't find someone to buy a boat with me, I'll have to _____ a loan.

13. I saw some statistics recently on the growing number of alcoholics in this country. The figures are _____.

14. A gift shop has a sign under its toy animal display that reads: "Don't feed the animals. They're already _____."

15. When a torrential rain submerged the playing field with water, the coach sent in his _____.

16. There are a lot of _____ characters in the lamp manufacturing business.

17. Coalminers who wear illuminated helmets do not have to drink hard liquor to get high. They're already _____.

18. A few years ago the oil exporting countries had the United States and Western Europe over a _____.

19. Any man who wants to wear a natural-looking, well-fitted hairpiece will have _____ a lot of money for it.

20. A golfer who gets hungry while playing 18 holes will always carry a _____ _____ in his bag.

21. A person who drives an ice cream truck on weekends might be called a _____ driver.

22. Many reporters start out working in ice cream parlors to learn how to get the _____.

23. Most people do not realize that Adam never had a _____ with Eve — only an apple.

24. A social climbing American pursued and married a wealthy English duke. She loves him for his

    _____ .

25. Around Christmas time, vegetarians send each other cards that read: "_____ on Earth."

Complete the puns below by choosing appropriate words from the following list. Some puns require more than one word. (No word in the list should be used more than once. Some words will not be used at all.)

appeal	imprint	recluse
big	intense	red
buffs	joint	richest
cent	knead	rip
clearance	lien	ruble
clip	milk	sausage
clothes	mutter	seam
curd	negligent	sham
develop	off	shorts
drawers	out	single
enlarge	outdoors	Sundays
enthusiasts	pain	surgeon
ferrous	pair	unsuited
granite	photographed	wait
happen	pieces	warm
impression	prints	weekends

26. A hypochondriac's favorite drink is _____

    _____ .

27. People who get stoned often are taken for

    _____ .

28. A Senator who regularly joins filibusters in the U.S. Senate likes to throw his _____ around.

29. People in the underwear business might refer to two illustrators as a _____ of _____.

30. Production costs can be high in the dairy business. A lot of expenses are in _____.

31. In comparison to other metal merchants, scrap dealers are among the _____.

32. Many tailors _____ to be making a good living.

33. My doctor has become a specialist in hip replacement operations. You might say he's _____ ahead in his field.

34. A photographer once brought his attractive female assistant into the darkroom to see what would _____.

35. If a Russian loses all his money, he'll be left without a _____ _____.

36. A photographer interviewed a number of bathing beauties to pose for a men's magazine. Some of the women were _____ for the job.

37. If an attorney wants to be successful, he tries not to lose his _____.

38. A notary public will always keep his seal in perfect working condition if he wants to make a good _____.

39. When I get fed up with my wife's constant grumbling, I send her home to _____.

40. Bakers _____ to make lots of dough.

41. Photographers make a good living by
_____.

42. People who go on camping trips are usually
_____ people.

43. When a well-known Caribbean resort became a
nudist retreat, the resort's apparel shop decided to
have a _____-_____ sale.

44. A hermit who drives carelessly and damages public
property can be charged with _____ driv-
ing.

45. You might say that a nude beach has a number of
sunbathing _____.

46. I was once served a pizza with 15 different top-
pings. I never _____ a spicy pizza.

47. A barbershop that charges $25 for a haircut is a
real _____ _____.

48. Collection attorneys are the most insecure members
of the profession; they're always looking for someone to _____ on.

49. When the Star Wars jigsaw puzzles first came out,
children all over the country went to
_____.

50. Stores sell most of their tanning oil on
_____.

GO ON TO PART 2

PART 2

Complete the puns for the illustrations below by filling in the missing words:

EXAMPLE:

Buffalo sanctuaries in the United States celebrate their 200th anniversary with a *Bisontennial* celebration.

Illustration by Rand Kington

1. A secretary fell madly in love with a janitor in her office building. He _____ her off her feet.

2. Many successful dermatologists had to build their practice from _____.

3. When a cook is having a bad day, he can easily blow his _____.

Illustrations by Rand Kington

4. I know a man who has worked as a chauffeur for 25 years and has nothing to _____ _____ it.

5. The most vulnerable animal in the world has to be a frog because if you just touch it, it will _____.

Illustrations by Rand Kington

6. A snail once painted large "S's" on his fast sports car so when he would drive down the street, people would say, "Look at that S car _____."

7. I know an artist who specializes in obscene oil portraits. His paint is made from _____ oil.

8. The salesman who sells padded bras from door to door is often referred to as the _____ bust man.

9. At an OPEC celebration party a few years ago, some of the guests were dancing _____ to _____.

10. A couple of ghosts walked into a tavern and asked the bartender if _____ were served in his establishment.

Illustrations by Rand Kington

11. When a new gyros restaurant opened and became popular, the submarine place across the street lost a lot of business and went _____.

12. A number of call girls have been recruited by the CIA. They work as _____ agents.

13. Never go into the cattle-raising business. You might get a _____ _____.

14. Sharks are overwhelmingly of one nationality — _____.

Illustrations by Rand Kington

15. When someone dropped a birth control pill into our photocopier, the machine would not _____.

16. A good-looking young actor was persuaded by his agent to model nude for a women's magazine. The agent felt his client needed the _____.

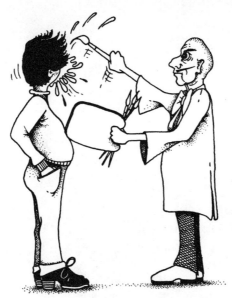

17. If an artist meets someone he doesn't like, he will give him the _____.

18. A special drink is made in Mexico by dipping a certain kind of bird into a glass of tequila. The drink is called "tequila _____."

Illustrations by Rand Kington

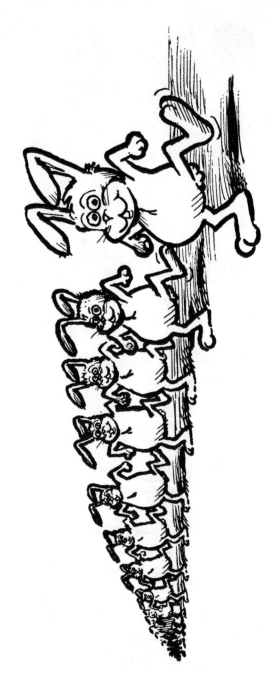

19. What do you have when a line of rabbits all take one step backwards at the same time?
A _____ hare line, of course.

Illustration by David Levi

20. A pick pocket eventually got caught stealing pocket watches because he took too much _____.

GO ON TO PART 3

PART 3

Complete the puns below by filling in the appropriate words. There is one blank space for each missing word.

EXAMPLE:
The last time I got a flat on my car I went into the house and put on my changing _attire_.

1. A traveling circus once hired an accountant away from a large public accounting firm. They heard he was good at _____ the books.

2. A country and western bar recently had a mechanical bull-riding contest. The winner ended up with a hundred _____.

3. Winter jackets made from goose feathers must always be on sale. Their sale tags are marked _____.

4. The best way to stop an elephant from _____ is to take away his credit card.

5. A golfer should always carry a third sock in his golf bag in case he gets a _____ in one.

6. A woman bought a jogging machine and got lots of use from it during the winter months. You might say she got more than a _____ for her money.

7. A man received a birthday present from his three golfing partners. They all _____ in for the gift.

8. A woman went to a party with a well-dressed, Olympic sprinter and told him he looked
_____.

9. A lady put some steaks in her freezer between the ice trays. That night her family had _____ steaks for dinner.

10. Well-behaved electrical engineering students try to _____ themselves properly in class at all times.

11. Apparently, there are a number of comedians who believe in public nudity. Just about everyone has seen a comic _____.

12. Two Californians pooled their resources to buy a secluded parcel of land to grow marijuana plants. You might describe their land purchase as a _____ venture.

13. To the Russians Lenin's tomb is a special place; to Americans it's just another Communist
_____.

14. The physician told his sick patient to quit smoking immediately and wanted no if's, and's or
_____.

15. Some deer do not have any doe. Others have a couple of _____.

16. Many female dressmakers see a psychologist on a regular basis to deal with seam _____.

17. For adult rabbits, bringing up an offspring is a hare-_____ experience.

18. A movie studio that makes a number of expensive flops will find itself in _____ trouble.

19. I know a janitor who once changed an electric bulb on the top floor of the Sears Tower in Chicago. He considers the event the _____ of his career.

20. Lumberjacks try to keep track of how many _____ days there are until Christmas.

21. Years ago straw hats were very popular. You might say they once had their _____ day.

22. Electricians read their trade journals to keep up with _____ developments.

23. Some people think that money spent on an expensive belt is money gone to _____.

24. You might say that actors and actresses who have been married a number of times have developed _____ egos.

25. Two leopards could easily get into a fight while playing if one called the other a _____.

26. A bull that spends a lot of time sleeping on the farm might be sold to a construction company as a _____.

27. There is a popular horse-breeding magazine that always features a monthly center _____.

28. If someone steals a goat's offspring from a farm, he could be charged with _____.

29. The state that produces most of the pencils in the United States is _____.

30. The calendar girls of the 1950's had to be very insecure. They knew their days were _____.

31. Unhappy consumers have been _____ about high meat prices for a long time.

32. A company that produces laundry soap recently went bankrupt. You might say they're all _____ _____.

33. Garbage collectors tend to be depressed most of their working careers. They're always down in the _____.

34. When an apartment building landlord calculates his expenses, he treats roof maintenance as _____.

35. A business school graduate decided to go to work for a successful perfume company, which makes a lot of _____.

36. The doctor injected a number of different medications into the ailing patient, but they were all in _____.

37. Two podiatrists in the same town might end up being _____ rivals.

38. People who are forced to eat a fish diet to survive have lots of _____ to pick.

39. Apathetic owls just don't give a _____.

40. If some strawberries weren't so fresh, they would not be in a ＿＿＿＿＿＿ today.

41. Few people realize how many products are derived from the coconut. It's a lot more than it's ＿＿＿＿＿＿ ＿＿＿＿＿＿ to be.

42. When people barbeque at a nude beach, they always make ＿＿＿＿＿＿ steaks.

43. A toothless termite went into a tavern, crawled up to the bar and asked, "Is the bar ＿＿＿＿＿＿ here?"

44. When an unmanned Russian spacecraft crashed onto the surface of Mars instead of making a soft landing, the Russians were unhappy because they did not ＿＿＿＿＿＿ that way.

45. An attorney will carry a small portfolio to court when he only has a ＿＿＿＿＿＿ case.

46. The trapped prison escapees told the sheriff's police that they would throw their hostages over the cliff; however, it was only a ＿＿＿＿＿＿.

47. The best country in the world for buying men's neckware is ＿＿＿＿＿＿.

48. The richest country in the world is Ireland because its capital is always ＿＿＿＿＿＿.

49. At the beach a bathing beauty is a girl worth ＿＿＿＿＿＿ for.

50. The money made from the sale of backyard badminton and volleyball sets could be described as ＿＿＿＿＿＿ profit.

51. A dentist in the army got busted for improper conduct from captain to _____ sergeant.

52. A navy surgeon who performs hemorrhoid operations might be called a _____ admiral.

53. A horse trainer will never have trouble getting a bank loan because he has a _____ job.

54. Sugar producers have been unhappy about low sugar prices for a long time. They have been raising _____ for years.

55. Some parents believe that swatting a naughty youngster over their knee is an important part of _____ a child.

56. A baseball fan will not be able to buy a bottle of beer at the ball park if the home team loses its _____.

57. Getting athlete's foot after losing a tough tennis match could be described as the agony of _____.

58. When a jockey gets married, he always checks into the _____ suite at a hotel.

59. When we are invited to a friend's new home for the first time, we often bring a portable heater as a _____ gift.

60. I'm sure you've heard about the timid stone that wanted to be a little _____.

61. One might consider a grandfather clock to be an old _____.

62. When pornographic movie actors are out of work, you could say they are among the _____ unemployed.

63. Many international playboys have been recruited into our diplomatic service; they're experienced in foreign _____.

64. A friend of mine has had a number of unusual problems with his car over the past five years. I told him he should write an _____-biography.

65. The ice cream parlor is one place where the consumer wants to get more than a fair _____.

66. If a student misses one of his tests at a school of cosmetology, he can always take a _____ exam.

67. Birth control clinics try to provide information for every _____ occasion.

68. Publishers have learned that a book does not have to be about internal medicine to have an

_____.

69. A woman who is anxious to conceive and imagines the symptoms of a pregnancy that has not occurred is laboring under a _____.

70. Bankers have a difficult time understanding why a woman without principle will draw a lot of

_____.

GO ON TO PART 4

PART 4

Create puns for the following situations in the time allotted below:

EXAMPLE:
You are out to dinner at an Italian restaurant with your spouse and another couple, enjoying a bottle of red wine with your meal. The waiter is going around the table refilling everyone's wine glass. When he comes to your side, you put your hand over your glass to indicate that you do not want a refill, but at that exact moment someone at another table distracts the waiter's attention and he pours wine all over your hand. As you wipe off your hand, think of an appropriate pun to fit the situation. (Time: 5 minutes)

Possible Response: *I pay attention to what I'm doing. Why Chianti?*

1. Let's say you have been invited to a party and are involved in a serious discussion with other guests about recent anti-handgun legislation across the nation. While the other guests are espousing arguments for and against handgun control, think of a clever pun to work into the conversation that will almost certainly leave you standing alone in the corner. (Time: 5 minutes)

2. You have been fixed up on a date and are having lunch at a restaurant. Your date mentions how she went shopping that morning and spent a fortune on clothes. She says, "You wouldn't believe how expensive designer jeans are!" Come up with an appropriate pun that could put the rest of the afternoon in jeopardy. (Time: 5 minutes)

3. Let's say that as a notorious punster you are being interviewed by *Proctology Today,* a well-known national magazine that has taken an interest in you because they consider you a real pain in the rear end. In the course of the discussion the interviewer talks about some of the distinguished proctologists in the country today. Think of an appropriate pun to work into the interview at an opportune moment. (Time: 10 minutes)

4. You are taking a world history course and are covering the French Revolution. The teacher comments about how many French noblemen were executed by the Revolution, and how the guillotine was an innovative and relatively quick method of death compared to the older methods of burning at the stake, torture, etc. Think of a pun to interject that will make the class laugh and surely cause the teacher to remember your name. (Time: 5 minutes)

5. Let's say your bosses at work invite you to join them for lunch. After a brief discussion of office matters, the conversation shifts to a discussion of the economy, world affairs and then the merits of an all-volunteer army. One of your bosses states that the major problem with an all-volunteer army is the shortage of qualified military personnel. Think of a pun to work into the conversation that could threaten your job security. (Time: 5 minutes)

Think of a good pun about each of the following subjects: (Time: 10 minutes per subject.)

EXAMPLE:
football: *A football player, who worked as a barber in the offseason, recently was forced to retire from the game. He was called too many times for clipping.*

6. lawyers: _____

_____

_____

7. dating: _____

_____

_____

8. dieting: _____

_____

_____

9. jogging or running: _____

_____

_____

10. the military: _____

_____

_____

11. baseball: _____

_____

_____

12. dogs: _____

_____

_____

13. farming: _____

_____

_____

14. fruit: _____

_____

_____

15. accountants: _____

_____

_____

16. music/dancing: _____

_____

_____

17. basketball: _____

_____

_____

18. underwear: _____

_____

_____

19. bakers: _____

_____

_____

20. skiing: _____

_____

_____

21. tennis: _____

_____

_____

22. dentists: _____

_____

_____

23. cars: _____

_____

_____

24. hotels: _____

_____

_____

25. gambling: _____

_____

_____

GO ON TO PART 5 (Optional)

PART 5 (Optional)

Create humorous illustrations for the following puns:

1. Skunks must pray a great deal. They each have their own pew.

2. A talent scout for a major league baseball team was holding tryouts for relief pitchers from the Mexican league and did a double take when two matadors showed up at the field. They heard the team was looking for experience in the bull pen.

3. My neighbor has a lot of crab grass in his lawn this year. In fact, his lawn is so crabby that when he sprinkles it, it spits water back at him.

4. After thoroughly chewing on a tree, a beaver took his leave by saying, "It's been nice gnawing you."

5. I know someone who cleans chimneys for a living. It soots him very well.

TEST ANSWERS AND SCORING

Part 1 Answers

1. materialistic
2. stirrup
3. petal
4. disguise
5. cleaners
6. meteor
7. paradox
8. capsizes
9. press
10. tie
11. mist
12. float
13. staggering
14. stuffed
15. subs
16. shady
17. lightheaded
18. barrel
19. to pay (toupee)
20. sand wedge
21. sundae
22. scoop
23. date
24. manors
25. peas
26. sham pain
27. granite
28. wait
29. pair drawers
30. curd
31. ferrous
32. seam
33. surgeon
34. develop
35. red cent
36. unsuited
37. appeal
38. impression
39. mutter
40. knead
41. enlarge
42. intense
43. clothes out
44. recluse
45. buffs
46. sausage
47. clip joint
48. lien
49. pieces
50. Sundays

Part 2 Answers

1. swept
2. scratch
3. stack
4. show for
5. croak
6. go (escargot)
7. crude
8. fuller
9. sheik sheik
10. spirits
11. under
12. undercover
13. bum steer
14. Finnish
15. reproduce
16. exposure
17. brush
18. mockingbird
19. receding
20. time

Part 3 Answers

1. juggling (or balancing)
2. bucks
3. down
4. charging
5. hole
6. run
7. chipped (or pitched)
8. dashing
9. cube
10. conduct
11. strip
12. joint
13. plot
14. butts (or but's)
15. bucks
16. stress
17. raising
18. reel (or real)
19. highlight
20. chopping
21. hay
22. current
23. waist (or waste)
24. alter
25. cheetah
26. bulldozer
27. foal
28. kidnapping
29. Pennsylvania
30. numbered
31. beefing
32. washed up
33. dumps
34. overhead
35. scents (or sense or cents)
36. vein (or vain)
37. arch
38. bones
39. hoot
40. jam
41. cracked up
42. strip
43. tender
44. planet
45. brief
46. bluff
47. Thailand
48. Dublin
49. wading (or waiting)
50. net
51. drill
52. rear
53. stable
54. Cain (or cane)
55. rearing
56. opener
57. defeat
58. bridal
59. house-warming
60. boulder
61. timer
62. hardcore
63. affairs
64. auto
65. shake
66. makeup
67. conceivable
68. appendix
69. misconception
70. interest

Compare your answers for Parts 1, 2 and 3 to those stated above. Score one point for each correct answer in Part 1, two points for each correct answer in Part 2 and three points for each correct answer in Part 3.

Possible Answers for Part 4

1. I hear that the National Rifle Association is urging its members to wear short-sleeved shirts at all times. They believe in the right to bear arms.
2. Speaking of designer jeans, I heard rumors that Calvin Klein and Gloria Vanderbilt are thinking about getting married. If they do, their children would have designer genes.
3. I understand that proctologists and magicians have a lot in common. They're both masters of deceit.
4. I would still rather be burned at the stake than have my head cut off. A hot steak is always better than a cold chop.
5. One reason the military cannot attract a sufficient number of qualified men is the mandatory military haircut. To completely shave a man's head is shear nonsense.
6. Regardless of the size and complexity of an estate, a good probate attorney's motto will be: "Where there's a will, there's a way."
7. A woman tried to fix one of her girl friends up with a cab driver she knew, but he did not want to meter.
8. You might say that the founder of Weight Watchers is living off the fat of the land.
9. Last night I went running at midnight; I could not remember something I was going to do in the morning and wanted to jog my memory.
10. I know a woman officer in the army who never takes her meals with the other officers. She likes to mess with the enlisted men.

11. A sportswriter recently suggested that his city's major league baseball team should move to the Philippines after the team blew a big first-place lead late in the season. He thought the team should be renamed, "The Manilla Folders."

12. There is a hungry, newborn collie lost in our neighborhood who has been eating the watermelons in a neighbor's garden. He has been described as a little melancholy.

13. After a heavy rain destroyed his entire lettuce crop, the farmer had his family help him replant the crop with the encouraging statement, "Lettuce begin anew."

14. When one melon asked another to marry it, the second replied, "Yes, but I can't elope."

15. Old accountants never die; they just lose their balance.

16. You might say that hula dancing is an asset to Hawaiian music.

17. Many basketball players spend a great deal of time observing taxidermists in order to learn how to stuff.

18. A man and a woman who had not seen each other for a number of years ran into each other at the men's underwear section of a department store. It was a brief encounter.

19. I know a baker who decided to quit the business. He got tired of the dough and went on the loaf.

20. One of the top Norwegian skiers injured himself during the national ski championships. It was a slalom occasion.

21. A man and woman met at a tennis club and decided to rally for a while. As they approached the court, the woman asked, "Is that a new can?" The man looked down over his shoulder and replied, "No; it's the same one I've always had."

22. The oath that is hanging in my dentist's office is: "To seek the tooth, the whole tooth and nothing but the tooth, so help me God."
23. A number of automobile dealers have gone through rough times recently. I have heard some real Saab stories.
24. Hotels go out of their way to hire Inn-experienced people.
25. At first the house was winning everything at the roulette table, but after a while things took a turn for the bettor.

The above puns are only possible answers. Your puns can be equally valid responses. For the puns you thought of for Part 4, score yourself as follows:

    4 points for a good pun in the allotted amount of time
    3 points for a good pun in more than the allotted time
    2 points for a mediocre pun in the allotted amount
        of time
    1 point for a mediocre pun in more than the allotted
        amount of time
    0 points for failure to answer or to create a pun.

Be honest in evaluating your responses. A good pun is one that is clever and blends in with the given conversation or situation, or fits the designated subject. It is suggested that if possible, you get together with a fellow punster and help evaluate each other's answers to this part of the Test. However, you must be the one who ultimately assigns the appropriate number of points to your answers.

Part 5

I have not presented possible illustrations for the puns in this part of the Test in order to give full reign to the punster's imagination and creativity.

EVALUATION OF TEST RESULTS

Add up all of your points for Parts 1, 2, 3 and 4 of the Test. There are a possible 50 points for Part 1, 40 points for Part 2, 210 points for Part 3 and 100 points for Part 4.

If you scored a total of 350 points or more, you are to be congratulated. You have demonstrated exceptional ability as a punster. You have mastered the art of punning to the extent that you have the potential for losing friends and agonizing people.

If you scored at least 300 points, but less than 350, you have developed skills as a punster, but could benefit from more seasoning and exposure to puns. It is suggested that you review *PUNishment* and the collection of puns in this book.* It would also be desirable to watch some old Marx Brothers movies.

If you scored at least 225 points, but less than 300 points, you have punster potential but need some work to make it in a world of puns. It is suggested that you intensely study *PUNishment* and the puns in this book,* and keep an ongoing list of puns you come across while watching television, reading the newspaper, listening to the radio, etc., to help you become more familiar with puns.

If you scored less than a total of 225 points on the Test, punning does not appear to be your bag. You can still enjoy puns, but if you're looking for a hobby, you might want to try ballroom dancing or yodeling.

If, in addition to scoring well on Parts 1, 2, 3 and 4, you were able to create humorous illustrations for the puns in Part 5, you deserve another feather in your cap. You have added a new dimension to your punning ability and have the potential for being an illustrious punster.

---

* If you appreciate off-color humor, you should also review *Grime and PUNishment*.

While the PPT was designed to test and evaluate your readiness to face a world of puns, it was also intended to make you laugh. I hope you have enjoyed taking it.

Readers are invited to send their Test results with their five best puns for Part 4 and their three best illustrations for Part 5, along with any comments about the Test to The PPT, c/o The Punster's Press, P.O. Box 405, Glenview, Illinois 60025. A special PPT Reporting Form has been provided on the following page. All submitted material shall become the property of the author, and each person submitting his or her Test results, puns, illustrations and/or comments hereby gives Harvey C. Gordon permission to use or publish the same in any manner determined by him.

PPT REPORTING FORM

On my honor as a punster, my scores on Parts 1–4 of the PPT were as follows:

Part 1 _____

Part 2 _____

Part 3 _____

Part 4 _____

_____

Total _____

My best puns for Part 4 of the PPT were as follows (Limit to 5 best):

Question No.   Pun

(Over)

Copies of my illustrations for the following puns are enclosed (Limit to 3 best):

Circle: 1   2   3   4   5

I have the following comments about the PPT (Tell us which part(s) you liked best):

I understand that all of the above-mentioned material shall become the property of Harvey C. Gordon and that he shall have the right to use or publish my puns, illustrations, Test results and/or comments in any manner determined by him.

Respectfully submitted by

_____
(Signature)

_____
(Name: Please Print)

_____
(Address: Please Print)

_____

Mail this form to: The PPT, c/o The Punster's Press, P.O. Box 405, Glenview, Ill. 60025

If you enjoyed *PUNdemonium,* you can order additional copies for family and friends along with the following humor books from The Punster's Press:

PUNishment: The Art of Punning or How To Lose Friends and Agonize People (2d. Ed.) by Harvey C. Gordon. A $2.95 quality paperback (Warner Books, Inc., 1980). *PUNishment* uniquely combines a collection of over 400 puns with techniques for punning in everyday conversation. The collection is categorized by subject matter and includes special multilingual puns. The techniques, if mastered, will separate the true artist from the mere amateur. (Illustrated)

Grime and PUNishment: A Collection of Sexciting Puns by Harvey C. Gordon. A $3.95 quality paperback (Warner Books, Inc., 1981). *Grime and PUNishment* is an off-color collection of over 350 puns about sex, which adds a new, sexciting dimension to the art of punning. (Illustrated)

Order Form

Please send me the following books:

_____ copies of *PUNdemonium* at $3.95 per copy $_____

_____ copies of *PUNishment* (2d. Ed.) at $2.95 per copy $_____

_____ copies of *Grime and PUNishment* at $3.95 per copy $_____

I have added the following amounts for postage and handling:

75¢ per order *plus* 25¢ per book $_____

                                     Total: $_____

My check, *payable to The Punster's Press, P.O. Box 405, Glenview, Illinois, 60025* for the above total amount is enclosed.

Please send my book order to (Please Print):

Name _____

Street _____

City _____ State _____ Zip _____